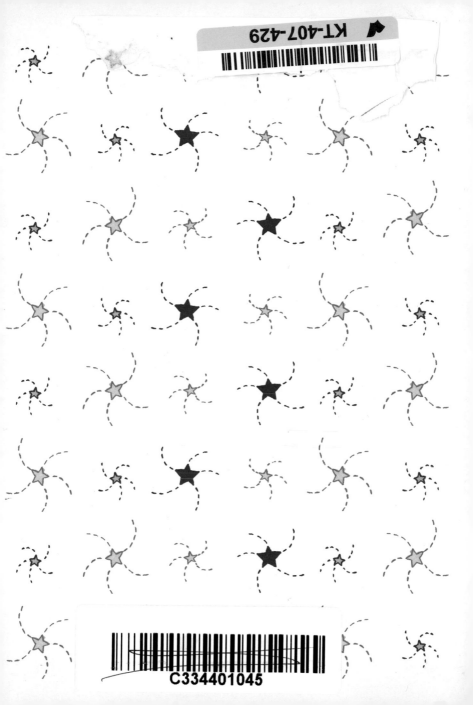

KT-407-429

C334401045

Five reasons why you'll love Isadora Moon...

Meet the magical,
fang-tastic Isadora Moon!

Isadora's cuddly toy, Pink Rabbit,
has been magicked to life!

Get ready to
enjoy the show!

Isadora's family is crazy!

Enchanting
pink and black
pictures

Dear Readers,

Sometimes we all feel like we don't fit in with the people around us, or that we can't do some things as well as other people can. Isadora Moon can't fly as quickly as other vampire children, and she can't do magic as well as other fairy children. There doesn't seem to be anyone else exactly like her.

But this is what makes her special. She is unique and magical in a way that is all her own—and so are you! There will be some things you can't do as well as some other people, and some things you can do better. There is also one thing you can do better than absolutely anyone else in the world, and that's being you!

I hope you enjoy reading about why being different makes Isadora Moon so special.

With love, magic and sparkle,
Harriet Muncaster x

What would you perform at a vampire talent show?

I would perform a fangtastic
garlic eating contest!!!
– Ellie

I'd attempt a vampire world record of
popping the most pink and black balloons
with my fangs in one minute!
– Violet

I would show how to make black frosted
cupcakes with enchanted bat wings.
– Leah

AcroBATics!
– Imogen

I would perform an act of
kindness to help spread good acts
around the world.
– Rafaela

I would fly like a vampire ballerina
because I love ballet so much.
– Jessica

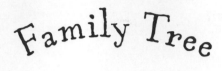

Family Tree

My Mum
Countess Cordelia
Moon

Baby Honeyblossom

My Dad
Count Bartholomew
Moon

Me!
Isadora Moon

Pink Rabbit

For vampires, fairies and humans everywhere!

And for my Granny and Grandpa.

OXFORD
UNIVERSITY PRESS

Great Clarendon Street, Oxford OX2 6DP

Oxford University Press is a department of the University of Oxford.
It furthers the University's objective of excellence in research, scholarship, and
education by publishing worldwide. Oxford is a registered trade mark of Oxford
University Press in the UK and in certain other countries

Copyright © Harriet Muncaster 2019
Illustrations copyright © Harriet Muncaster 2019

The moral rights of the author/illustrator have been asserted
Database right Oxford University Press (maker)

First published 2019

All rights reserved. No part of this publication may be reproduced,
stored in a retrieval system, or transmitted, in any form or by any means,
without the prior permission in writing of Oxford University Press,
or as expressly permitted by law, or under terms agreed with the appropriate
reprographics rights organization. Enquiries concerning reproduction outside
the scope of the above should be sent to the Rights Department, Oxford
University Press, at the address above

You must not circulate this book in any other binding or cover
and you must impose this same condition on any acquirer

British Library Cataloguing in Publication Data

Data available

ISBN: 978-0-19-276869-8

1 3 5 7 9 10 8 6 4 2

Printed in China

Paper used in the production of this book is a natural,
recyclable product made from wood grown in sustainable forests.
The manufacturing process conforms to the environmental
regulations of the country of origin.

ISADORA MOON

Puts on a Show

Harriet Muncaster

OXFORD
UNIVERSITY PRESS

Chapter ONE

'The nights are getting longer,' said Dad, peering out of the window at the dusky sky. 'It's almost time for the annual vampire ball!'

My dad is a vampire and he loves it when the evenings start to get darker and the air is crisp and cold.

'Your favourite event of the year!' said

Mum, who was busy watering her plants on the kitchen windowsill. My mum is a fairy (which makes me a vampire-fairy by the way!) and loves nature. Our house is always full of flowers.

'It is,' said Dad putting his arm around me. 'And this year it will be extra special. This year Isadora is old enough to go too!'

'I can't wait!' I said. 'And nor can Pink Rabbit. He *is* allowed to come, isn't he?' Pink Rabbit used to be my favourite stuffed toy but my mum magicked him alive with her wand. He comes everywhere with me.

'Of course,' said Dad, 'as long as he wears a proper vampire cape.'

'Oh goody!' I said, starting to feel excited.

Dad took a long suck of his red juice. Like all vampires, he only ever eats and drinks red food. 'There's one more thing,' he said. 'This year's ball is a bit more special than the other ones. It's going to be held on the night of a blood moon!'

'A blood moon!' I said, 'What's that?'

'It's when the moon is low in the sky,' said Mum, 'and the earth goes between the sun and the moon, which makes it glow red. It's very beautiful!'

'Yes,' said Dad. 'And there hasn't been a vampire ball on the night of a blood moon since I was a young boy. To celebrate, all the young vampire children have been asked to prepare a little show to perform in front of everyone. There's going to be a sort of talent contest!'

'A talent contest?' I said anxiously.

'Yes,' said Dad. 'But it's nothing to worry about. I'm sure you'll think of something really marvellous. And you can always do your performance with one of the other vampire children!'

'But I don't have any vampire friends,' I said. 'I go to a human school!'

'Ah, yes,' said Dad. 'Well, that's OK. You can just do your performance on your own. There will only be a couple of hundred vampires there.' He finished up his red juice with a noisy slurp.

'A couple of hundred!' I exclaimed, my heart starting to pitter-patter very fast. 'That's more than everybody in my school!'

'Pah!' said Dad, waving his hand in the air.

'You'll be great!' said Mum. 'And we'll all be there, cheering you on—Granny and Grandpa too! Maybe you could do a dance in your favourite black, starry tutu! You love ballet!'

'Hmm,' said Dad.

'What do you mean, "hmm"?' said Mum.

'Well, ballet isn't very vampire-y,' said Dad. 'When I did my performance many moons ago I showed off my teeth-brushing regime. Everyone was very interested to see how I keep my fangs so white and polished.'

'Were they?' asked Mum disbelievingly.

'Yes!' said Dad. 'We vampires love grooming, as you know.'

'I don't want to brush my teeth in front of two hundred vampires,' I said.

'Well, you don't have to do *that!*' said Dad. 'I'm sure you'll think of something else just as good!'

'Ballet!' I said. 'It's the thing I am best at! I won't be as nervous if I can do ballet.'

'Isadora is a wonderful dancer,' said Mum.

'She is,' agreed Dad. 'But . . .'

'Who cares if vampires don't do ballet?' said Mum. 'Isadora should do whatever she feels most comfortable doing.'

'Well, yes, I suppose,' said Dad.

'Great—thanks Dad!' I said. 'It will be good practice for when I am a proper ballerina!' I started to pirouette around the kitchen, twirling and spinning, finishing up with a low curtsy.

'Wonderful!' said Mum, clapping her hands.

'Bravo!' said Dad, smiling.

I left the kitchen and ran upstairs to my bedroom, Pink Rabbit hopping along behind me. I knew I was really good at ballet, but the thought of dancing in front of such a large audience was a bit daunting. I only had two weeks to practise my performance and I wanted it to be perfect.

'We have to show vampires how great ballet can be!' I said to Pink Rabbit, opening up my wardrobe and taking out my black starry tutu. I put it on and began to improvise, leaping, spinning, and twirling around the room. Pink Rabbit followed along behind me. The fairy dust from my tutu puffed up around us, creating sparkly clouds for us to dance through.

'I know!' I said, grabbing my wand from where it lay on the bed. 'Let's add some magic! Vampires don't have wands! It will be something different for them to see.' I waved my wand as I did a pirouette, and little fireworks crackled in the air.

I started to flap my wings, rising up towards the ceiling and doing a loop the loop. Pink Rabbit clapped his paws.

We carried on practising for the rest of the evening, until it was time to go to bed.

'It's going to be an amazing show!' I said confidently to Pink Rabbit as we snuggled down under my duvet together. 'I can't wait!'

The next morning at school I told my friends all about the talent contest.

'Two hundred vampires!' gulped Samantha, going a bit white. 'That's a lot of people looking at you!'

'It is!' nodded Sashi. 'I would be too scared to do that!'

'I wouldn't,' said Zoe. 'But that's because I'm going to be an actress when I grow up!'

'It's not that many,' I said, starting to feel a little nervous. 'My dad said it will be fine!'

'I'm sure it will be fine,' said Bruno. 'As long as you don't mess it up!'

'You're very brave!' said Jasper.

'Thanks,' I replied in a small voice.

'Of course Isadora won't mess up her dance,' said Zoe loudly. 'She's the best at ballet in our whole class!'

'Oh, definitely!' said Sashi. 'No one can dance as well as Isadora!'

Pink Rabbit jumped up and down and poked Sashi with his paw.

'Apart from Pink Rabbit of course!' said Sashi quickly.

Miss Cherry came into the room and we all went to sit down at our desks.

'What if I do?' I whispered to Zoe.

'Do what?' Zoe whispered back.

'Mess up my dance!' I said. 'What if it all goes wrong? Everyone will laugh at me!'

'It won't go wrong!' said Zoe. 'And even if it does it won't matter! Don't worry, Isadora. Don't listen to what anyone else says.'

But I couldn't help worrying. Now that the thought had occurred to me all I could think about was making a mistake during my special performance and I was remembering everything that Dad had said, about how ballet isn't very vampire-ish. What if nobody liked my dance? What if they thought it was silly? What if it was too *fairy-ish* for them? My cheeks started to get hot as I imagined the audience booing me off the stage. Maybe I should choose something else to perform? Something that the audience would definitely like. Something easy and safe where I couldn't make any mistakes.

'Can you help me, Dad?' I asked when I got home from school. 'I need a new idea for my performance. I don't want to do a ballet show anymore.'

'Why not?' said Mum. 'I thought you were really excited about it.'

'I was,' I said. 'But I've gone off it. I want to think of something else.'

'Of course I can help!' said Dad excitedly. 'How about a demonstration of you brushing your hair and making it all sleek and shiny like a proper vampire's hair? That would be great!'

'Hmm,' I said. Dad is always trying to get me to brush my hair. Vampires are very fond of grooming.

'I think it would be brilliant!' said
Dad. 'There would be a real contrast
between your usual—er—wild hairdo and
the new shiny sleek one!'

'It would be easy to do . . .' I said,
thinking about how brushing my hair on
stage couldn't possibly go wrong.

'Very easy!' said Dad.

'Wouldn't it be a little boring?' asked Mum.

'Not for vampires!' said Dad. 'They would love it! I know, let's do a practice now, Isadora. Why don't you go and get your hairbrush?'

'Oh . . .' I said. 'Maybe later. I have some homework to do.' I scooted quickly out of the kitchen and ran up the stairs to my bedroom.

For the next two weeks I didn't practise ballet once. The only time I wore my tutu was to my ballet lesson with Madame Giselle on Friday afternoon.

'You should tell her!' said Zoe as we put on our ballet shoes. 'About your show! She might give you some tips!'

'I've changed my idea,' I said. 'I'm not doing a ballet performance anymore.'

'Why not?' asked Zoe. 'It would be great! What are you doing instead then?'

'I'm going to—' I began, but just then Madame Giselle called us into the dance studio. 'I'll tell you later,' I said.

But later never came because Zoe got picked up early from the class and then it was the weekend. When I saw her on Monday morning we didn't discuss my performance because Zoe had got a new kitten and it was all she could talk about.

Every day that week, after school, I
opened my wardrobe door and stared at
my tutu shimmering in the light. But each
time I reached out my hand to get it out
and put it on, butterflies started to flutter
in my tummy and all I could hear was the
imaginary sound of hundreds of vampires
booing me off the stage. So I quickly
closed the door again and went to look in
the mirror instead. Brushing my hair
would be a safer option. Everybody at the
ball would like that.

Chapter TWO

'Today's the day!' yelled Dad on the
evening of the vampire ball. He had
got up especially early so that he would
have lots of time to get ready. 'My hair
must be as shiny as a mirror tonight!' he
said. 'Isadora, are you all ready for your
performance?'

'I think so,' I said, putting down my

piece of peanut butter on toast and suddenly not feeling very hungry anymore.

'If you like, you can borrow my great-great-great-grandfather's very special antique vampire comb,' said Dad. 'The rubies will flash wonderfully under the stage lights!'

'That's OK,' I said. 'I don't want to lose it.'

'You won't lose it,' said Dad. 'I'll keep it safe in my cape pocket and give it to you just before you go on stage!'

'OK,' I shrugged. I didn't really care what I used for my act. I just wanted to get it over with. Just then Mum came into the room wearing a black vampire cape. It felt strange to see her in it. She only has one cape and gets it out once a year for the vampire ball.

'I wish it was pink,' she said. 'Pink is such a cheerful colour!'

'But not as cheerful as black!' said Dad happily. He was in an extremely good mood.

'What are you going to wear,

Isadora?' asked Mum. 'Let's go and find you something smart.' She led me back up to my bedroom and opened my wardrobe door.

'How about this?' she asked, taking out a long, velvet black dress with a white batwing collar.

'Maybe,' I said, staring at my tutu which twinkled all over with silver stars. I reached out my hand and stroked it. A cloud of fairy dust puffed up into the air.

'You could wear your tutu,' said Mum, 'if you like.'

'Really?' I said.

'I don't see why not,' said Mum. 'I

think the vampire ball could do with a
bit of fairy glitter.' She pulled it out and
handed it to me.

'Are you sure you don't want to do your ballet show?' she asked. 'It's not too late!'

'I'm sure,' I said.

'OK then,' said Mum, walking back towards my door. 'Don't forget to put your vampire cape on! And don't forget Pink Rabbit's either!'

By seven o'clock we were all ready and standing by the front door.

'We look marvellous!' said Dad. 'Very gothic!' He patted his cape pocket. 'I've got the comb in here, Isadora,' he said. 'For when you need it!'

'Thanks, Dad,' I said quickly.

We all kissed my baby sister
Honeyblossom goodbye, waved to the
babysitter, and walked down the front
path. A long, sleek vampire taxi was
waiting by the gate. Dad opened the door
so that Mum and I could step in.

'Ooh!' he said. 'Velvet seats!'

We sped along the road and out into
the countryside. Once the driver was sure
there were no other cars on the road he
pressed a button on the dashboard. Big,
metal bat wings unfolded from either side

of the car and lifted it up into the sky and towards the stars. We glided through the air, zooming fast over rivers and lakes that shimmered in the red moonlight.

'We really ought to get our car fitted with wings,' said Dad, peering out of the window. 'You know, for going abroad and stuff.'

'But we don't ever go abroad,' said Mum.

'We might,' said Dad, 'if we had a car with wings!'

Pink Rabbit and I stared out of the window, watching the tiny houses and roads below. There were only a few dotted about now and soon there were none at all.

'We're deep in the countryside.' said Dad. 'Look how brightly the stars are shining! And there's the Milky Way!'

'Beautiful!' sighed Mum. 'Just

beautiful!'

Pink Rabbit and I gazed up at the sky. The stars were so dazzling that they illuminated the craggy dark mountains below.

'What's that?' I asked, spotting a tall, spindly building at the top of the tallest mountain. Spires and turrets twisted upwards, and hundreds of tiny arched windows shone with an eerie red light.

'The vampire castle!' cried Dad. 'It's where we're going!'

The taxi glided gracefully towards the castle, landing with a gentle bump on the long driveway leading up to the front doors.

'Wow!' I whispered, staring up at it
looming above us. 'It's so big!'

'Vampire headquarters!' said Dad proudly as he stepped out of the taxi. All around us other vampires were stepping out of cars, their black capes billowing in the night breeze.

'Let's go in!' said Dad.

We walked towards the tall front doors of the castle. Dad showed our tickets to a skinny vampire with a pale face and the longest fangs I had ever seen.

'Do come in,' he said. We stepped over the threshold and into a big hall with a grand staircase in it and huge chandeliers hanging from the ceiling. They were lit with real candles that dripped with wax, the flames flickering red

and dancing over the walls of the room.

'Spectacular!' said Dad.

Pink Rabbit and I stood in the middle of the floor and stared in awestruck wonder.

'Come on!' said Dad. 'This is only the entrance hall!' He beckoned us to follow him towards a pair of doors which led into another room. As we walked he nodded and waved to lots of vampire friends that he knew. We went past a row of very ornate vampire portraits, under another dripping, flickering chandelier, and then

into the great ballroom.

'Wow!' I said again, stopping in my tracks. This room was enormous. The ceiling was made from one giant mirror, and even bigger, fancier chandeliers hung down from it. Vampire waiters were circling around with trays of red canapés to snack on and tall glasses of red juice to drink.

All around us other vampires milled around and chatted. Capes swished from every direction—black silk and midnight velvet. There was music playing and

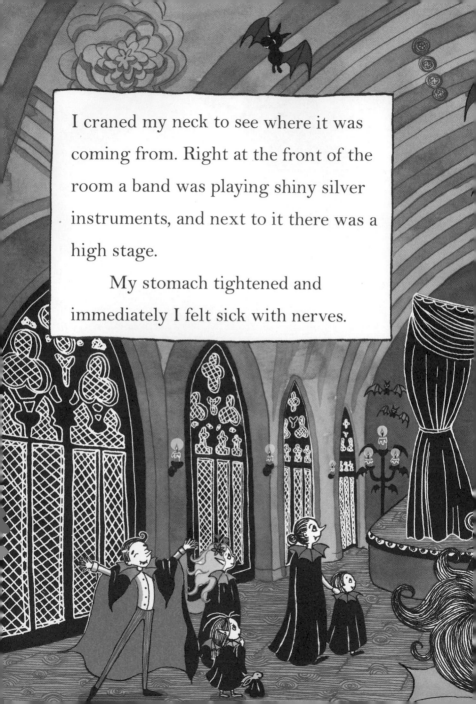

I craned my neck to see where it was coming from. Right at the front of the room a band was playing shiny silver instruments, and next to it there was a high stage.

My stomach tightened and immediately I felt sick with nerves.

I didn't want to stand up in front of all these vampires and perform something. Suddenly I wished I had stayed at home with Honeyblossom and the babysitter. I tugged on Mum's dress.

'Mum!' I said. 'Mum!'

'What is it?' asked Mum.

'Can we go home?'

'Go home!' snorted Dad, overhearing. 'You make the funniest jokes, Isadora! We've only just got here!'

'I'm not joking,' I said. 'I want to go home!'

Dad's face took on a serious expression. 'What's the matter?' he asked. 'Do you feel ill?'

'Sort of,' I mumbled, glancing at the stage.

'Oh!' said Mum. 'I think I know what the problem is. Isadora, you don't *have* to perform anything if you really don't want to.'

'That's right,' said Dad, sounding slightly disappointed. 'If you *really* don't want to you don't have to but—'

'Bartholomew!' came a sudden cry from behind us and we all turned around.

'Mother!' said Dad.

'Granny and Grandpa!' I shouted, running forward to hug them.

'How lovely to see you here this year,' said Granny, wrapping me in her black satin cape that was studded all over with tiny diamonds. 'I am so looking forward to your performance!'

'Me too!' said Grandpa, smiling so that his fangs flashed bright white in the candlelight. 'Fancy! Our little Isadora up on the stage!'

'Oh . . .' I said. 'I . . .'

'You're going to be absolutely marvellous,' said Granny, letting me go.

'A real treat!' said Grandpa. 'What are you going to perform? No, wait! Don't tell me. I'd like it to be a surprise!'

I smiled at my grandparents both with their perfectly coiffured hair and sharp shiny fangs. I couldn't bear to tell them that I didn't want to perform. I decided not to say anything. Grandpa often dozed off while watching things anyway. Maybe they wouldn't notice.

'Mum, Dad!' I said once my grandparents were distracted with some old friends that had appeared nearby.

'I really don't want to go on stage. I'm not doing it!'

'But—' began Dad.

'No!' I said. 'You can't make me!'

Then I ran off into the crowd, my eyes feeling all prickly.

Chapter THREE

Vampires stood in their black capes
all around me and with all the candles
burning everywhere the room felt
very hot. I made my way back into the
entrance hall where the air felt cooler
and noticed a group of vampire children
about my age standing near the bottom
of the staircase. They were chatting

excitedly and showing off to each other, zooming up into the air and chasing each other around the room.

'No flying indoors!' the vampire doorman shouted at them but no one listened. They were having too much fun. I stood back and watched for a while. They all looked very smart and neat with polished shoes and hair that glinted in the candlelight. But then I noticed one of them who didn't look quite the same. She was sitting a little way away on the bottom step of the staircase and watching the other children wistfully. She didn't look happy or excited at all.

'I wonder what the matter with that one is,' I said to Pink Rabbit, pointing. He shrugged.

'Why don't you hop over to her,' I said, 'and then I can follow you!'

Pink Rabbit blinked his button eyes and folded his arms across his chest.

'Oh please!' I said. 'I feel too shy to go over to her myself!'

Pink Rabbit sighed and began to hop over to where the little vampire girl was sitting, his little cape flapping out behind him. I hurried after him.

'Pink Rabbit!' I said out loud. 'Where are you going? That's the wrong

way to the ballroom!' Pink Rabbit turned
around and stared at me, putting his hands
on his hips and shaking his head. I felt
my cheeks turn pink but we were at the
bottom of the stairs now and very close to
the vampire girl.

'The ballroom's that way,' she said, pointing.

'Erm, thank you,' I said and made as if to walk away but Pink Rabbit pulled at the bottom of my cape and stamped his foot.

'Is that a tutu?' asked the vampire girl, seeing it peeping out from under my cape.

'Yes!' I said. 'A ballet tutu!'

'Oh!' said the vampire girl, and a funny look came over her face. 'I thought vampires didn't do ballet.'

'We don't!' shouted a little vampire boy who was flying up in the air nearby and doing a very smart loop the loop.

'Ballet is too flowery for vampires,' said another girl who was sucking red juice out of a fancy glass bottle with a straw.

'Too pink and flouncy,' said the boy.

'Too bright and sparkly,' said another.

'Too fairy-ish!'

'Too human!'

'Oh,' I said and
felt very, very glad
that I hadn't decided to
do my ballet performance
that night. I pulled my cape more tightly
around me to hide my tutu and sat down
on the stairs next to the vampire girl.

'I'm Isadora,' I said. 'And this is Pink
Rabbit. What's your name?'

'Araminta,' said the girl. A waiter
passed by us and held out a tray of
canapés—tiny red spongy things on
sticks.

'Oh, no thank you,' said Araminta

and her face went green. I took one to be
polite and put it down on the step next to
me.

'Don't you like red food?' I asked in
surprise. 'All vampires like red food!'

'I don't,' said Araminta. 'And it looks
like you don't either! You've put it down
on the step.'

'Oh well . . .' I said, wondering if I
should tell her the truth or not. The other
children were too busy laughing and
flying about to listen so I leaned in close

and whispered in Araminta's ear, 'I'm not a full vampire. I'm half fairy!'

'You're what?' cried Araminta, jumping up and staring at me.

'Shh!' I said, pulling her back down. 'Don't shout about it!'

'Sorry,' said Araminta. 'But I've never met another half vampire before! I'm half vampire too!'

'You are?' I said in surprise. 'Really?'

'Yes,' said Araminta. 'My mum's a vampire but my dad's a human! I have fangs and I can fly but I absolutely hate red food and I'm scared of the dark!'

'I hate red food too!' I said excitedly. 'This is so great! I've never met another half vampire before! Where do you go to school?'

'I go to a human one,' said Araminta.

'Me too!'

Araminta stared at me with happy sparkling eyes and I stared back. It felt so special to find someone else like me.

'I'm so glad you're here,' said Araminta. 'I'm not used to being surrounded by so many vampires. And I've been so scared about doing my performance. I've been worrying that it's too . . . human.'

'What is it?' I asked.

'A ballet show!' said Araminta. 'I love ballet so much. My dad said I should just

do the thing that makes me feel happy and
not worry about what anyone else thinks.
But now I'm here I feel really scared that
all the vampires will laugh at me.'

'You shouldn't worry about that!'
I said. 'You should do it if it's what you
want to do!'

'I know,' said Araminta. 'I'm going to. I'm just really nervous.'

'It will be fine!' I said, patting her on the knee. 'My mum told me that even the most famous dancers get nervous before they go on stage. Being nervous makes you perform better!'

'That makes me feel a bit better,' said Araminta. 'Thank you Isadora. What are you doing for your performance?'

'Oh . . .' I said and felt my face turn red. How could I tell Araminta that I wasn't brave enough to do a performance at all—especially not the one I really wanted to do?

'Are you doing a ballet show too?'

asked Araminta. 'Is that why you're wearing a tutu? I've got mine on. Look!'

'Well . . .' I said. 'I was going to do a ballet show but . . .' I stared at Araminta's tutu and at the tiny silvery bats scattered all over the puffy black skirt. I thought about the advice I had just given her. Suddenly I felt very silly for not doing the thing I really wanted to do just because I was afraid of what people would think. Why couldn't I just be myself? I wanted to be brave like Araminta.

'Yes!' I said. 'I'm doing a ballet show too!' And I lifted my cape to show Araminta my very special black glittering tutu.

'That's so great!' said Araminta,
hugging me. 'I won't be the only one!'

'Let's show all those vampires how
elegant and gothic ballet can be!' I said.

We smiled at each other and then Araminta said, 'I've got an idea! Why don't we do our show together? We could make it twice as amazing that way!'

'Yes!' I replied, feeling my heart soar. 'What a perfect idea!'

'We need to practise then!' said Araminta, taking my hand and leading me to a quiet place behind the staircase in the entrance hall. Pink Rabbit bounced along behind.

'Let me see your dance routine,' said Araminta, 'and then I'll show you mine!'

'OK,' I said. 'Come on, Pink Rabbit, you're in it too!' I stretched out my arms

and pointed my foot. Then I
began to spin and swirl and leap.
It felt so good to be dancing
again. I was good at ballet. I
should never have thought of
doing anything else!

'Wow!' said Araminta when I had
finished. 'I love the fireworks! They're
so pretty!' Then she began to dance
and I watched her transform
from a vampire-human into a
graceful ballerina.

'You have some great
moves!' I said. 'Can you teach me some
of them?'

'Of course!' said Araminta.

For the next hour we practised a new routine together. It was the most fun I had had in ages.

'I can't wait to show my ballet teacher at home,' I said to Araminta as we made our way back into the grand ballroom. It looked completely different in there now with rows and rows of velvet chairs set up facing the stage. Vampires were beginning to take their seats all over the room. I could see my family sitting in a row near the front.

'We'd better go and sit down,' said Araminta.

'Yes,' I said. 'I'll see you later!'

Chapter FOUR

'There you are!' said Mum when I scurried into the row of seats and sat down next to her. 'Where have you been?'

'I met a friend,' I said.

'Lovely!' said Mum. 'And don't worry about the performance. I've told the organizers of the ball to take your name off the list. You won't be called up to perform anything.'

'Oh . . .' I said. But then I remembered
that it didn't matter. Araminta and I had
agreed that we would both go up when
one of our names was called—whichever
one was called first. I decided not to tell
Mum and Dad. It would be a nice surprise
for them.

'Granny and Grandpa were a bit
disappointed,' whispered Mum as a gust of
wind blew through the ballroom, blowing
out the candles above our heads. 'But I
told them you would do a special little
show for them next time we visit.'

Just then the orchestra started up and
a bright light shone onto the stage.

A very distinguished-looking vampire
with a twirly moustache came prancing
into view.

'Welcome,' he said grandly, 'to the annual vampire ball!' There was a big cheer from the audience. 'How wonderful to see so many bright white fangs shining back at me! To celebrate the blood moon tonight, our little vampires are going to put on a show for us. We will see just how talented they all are! And there will be a few prizes for the best performances. So without further ado here is the first act. Introducing Nicholas Darkfang with his synchronized flying bats!'

There was another big cheer, and a vampire about my age walked confidently onto the stage, holding a tall wire cage. He opened the door of the cage and eight

bats fluttered out into the air
and arranged themselves into a circle
above Nicholas's head. Nicholas pulled a
thin black stick out from under
his cape and began to
wave it around like
a conductor. The
bats followed the stick
and began to fly up and down
alternately, making pretty
patterns in the air.

'Ooh!' said the audience.

'Ahh!' I held Pink Rabbit up so that he could see better.

Next onto the stage was another vampire boy who was wearing a pair of black-rimmed spectacles.

'I am going to show you how to make the best vampire hair gel in the world!' he said, opening up a suitcase and getting out all sort of bottles and test tubes. He began to pour and stir. There was a lot of smoke and then a loud bang.

'Here we are!' he said, holding out a little glass bottle with some green goop in the bottom of it. He poured some onto his hand and smoothed it onto his hair.

'Wow!' said the audience as the vampire boy's hair gleamed under the stage lights.

'I need some of that!' I heard Dad say.

Next came a group of three vampire children who did a flying display, shooting upwards into the air and soaring around the ballroom so fast that they became a blur.

'Gosh!' said Dad with his hand over his mouth. 'Times have changed since I did my performance! The hair-brushing routine might have been a little boring after all.'

I watched and felt the butterflies in my tummy get stronger and stronger. I wondered when it would be my turn to go up.

'Now,' said the host after the three vampires had finished their flying display, 'we have something a little different!' I held my breath. 'Araminta Smith is going to perform some "ballet" for us!'

90

There was an interested murmuring in the audience and I saw Araminta stand up from her chair at the other side of the room. She glanced over at me and I stood up too.

'What are you doing?' asked Mum. 'Do you need to go to the bathroom?'

'No,' I told her. 'I've got a surprise for you!'

'A surprise!' said Dad eagerly. 'Do you need the comb?'

I shook my head and waved at my parents and grandparents as I made my way along the row of seats. I was pleased to see that Grandpa was still awake and smiling excitedly. Pink Rabbit and I hurried over to where Araminta was waiting at the bottom of the stage steps.

'Break a leg!' she whispered to me.

'What?' I asked, shocked.

'It's what all the actors and dancers say to each other!' she said as we walked up the steps together. 'It means good luck!'

'Oh right,' I said. 'I hope you break a leg too then!'

Now we were on the stage with the bright lights shining on us. I couldn't even see the audience properly from up there They were all a dark blur. I took a deep breath and closed my eyes as I got into my starting position. I would pretend I was just in my bedroom with Pink Rabbit, dancing for my dolls and teddies. Music started to play and I felt a tingling in my feet. I leapt up into the air, lifting both my feet as high as they would go. As I opened my eyes I saw Araminta doing the same. We began to dance together, keeping in time to the music as best we could, spinning and twirling and somersaulting.

I waved my wand and sent little fireworks
crackling and sparkling over the heads
of everyone in the audience. I heard a
collective gasp and an 'ooh' and an 'ah'. I
felt as though there were fireworks inside
me too—it felt amazing to be up on stage
doing the thing that I like doing most in
the world. I couldn't believe I had almost
not done it at all. I didn't even care if the
audience liked our dance or not—I loved
it and Araminta was surely loving it too.
She had a smile on her face as wide as a
crescent moon.

When we finished we did a low
curtsy and I made bat-shaped sequins
appear in the air with my wand which

rained down on top of us. There was silence for a few moments and I searched for my family through the haze of lights. They were all sitting there with their mouths open, looking gobsmacked. I gulped. Suddenly there was a roar from the audience and everybody started clapping. Some vampires even stood up!

'We did it!' said Araminta breathlessly and hugged Pink Rabbit and me.

'Thank you!' boomed the host's voice from a microphone, and he came walking back onto the stage. 'What an interesting and unusual performance!'

Araminta and I couldn't stop smiling.

Together we stepped back down off

the stage and I ran over to where Mum
and Dad and my grandparents were
sitting. Mum's mouth was still hanging
open and she was staring at me.

'Wow Isadora!' she said. 'Just wow!'

'What a stupendous surprise!' said
Granny, beaming.

'Fangtastic!' said Grandpa.

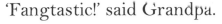

'Really wonderful!' said Dad. 'I'm so glad you didn't go with the hair-brushing routine in the end. This was much more YOU!'

I sat back down in my seat and waited for the next act. It was hard to concentrate on watching it though because I felt so proud and happy inside that I thought I might burst! I wanted to do it all over again! More vampires came on stage and did different things. There was a red juice-drinking contest and a pet bat who could do special tricks. By the time we got to the end it was very late.

'Now for the prizes!' said the host, coming back on stage with an armful of shiny silver bat-shaped trophies. 'The first award is for the slickest performance!' he said. 'It goes to Nicholas Darkfang for his wonderful display of synchronized bats!'

I watched as Nicholas hurried up onto the stage and took his trophy, bowing neatly.

'The next award is for the most informative performance,' said the host and awarded the prize to the vampire who had invented the hair gel.

'And the prize for the best overall performance is . . .' said the host—I held my breath—'Bella Stardash for her amazing pet bat tricks!'

There was a great 'whoop!' from the audience and lots of stamping of feet, and Bella Stardash ran up to the stage to collect her prize.

'Well done!' said the host. 'And we've decided to add one extra prize tonight too.' He pulled two smaller bat-shaped trophies out from inside his cape and held them up. 'A prize for the most unusual performance,' he said. 'Something we've never seen before—Araminta Smith and Isadora Moon's beautiful ballet show.'

I stared up at the stage in disbelief.

'Go on!' whispered Mum. 'Go and collect your prize!'

I stood up and made my way back up towards the stage. I could see Araminta making her way there too.

'Well done!' said the host, handing us both our prizes. 'I think we all enjoyed seeing something a little different! And who knows, maybe we'll start our own vampire ballet classes in the future! It *is* such an elegant and stylish style of dancing.'

I took my trophy and grinned at Araminta. This had turned out better than I could have hoped. Instead of being laughed at for doing something a bit different, we had won a prize!

'Now!' said the host. 'The show is over. Let's get back to the ball!'

The lights went down and suddenly all the candles burst back into flame. The orchestra started to play and the waiters busied about removing all the chairs in the room. Vampires all around us started ballroom dancing. I saw Mum and Dad take each other's hands and sway to the music. Dad grabbed my hand and pulled me in too, twirling me round and round and round.

'Stop, Dad!' I laughed. 'I'm dizzy!'

Once he had let me go I hurried back to Araminta and we did some more dancing together.

'Can you teach me some ballet?' came a voice from behind us. Araminta and I turned round to see the boy from the entrance hall earlier. The one who had said that ballet was too 'bright and sparkly' for vampires.

'Of course!' I said.

'We'd love to!' said Araminta.

As the music played we
showed some of the vampire
children how to point their feet
and pirouette and do a grand jeté
across the floor.

'It takes some practice,' said
Araminta and put her hand up to
her mouth to stifle a yawn. 'I'm
tired,' she said. 'I'm not used to
staying up all night.'

'Me neither,' I said. 'It's because we are both only half vampire!'

We smiled at each other and a flicker of understanding passed between us.

'Shall we have a nap?' I asked.

'I would love a nap!' said Araminta.

We made our way back to the entrance hall and to the place where we

had practised our dance earlier. I took off
my cape and laid it on the ground.

'Goodnight Araminta,' I said, lying
down on top of it.

'Night Isadora,' said Araminta.

I closed my eyes and, before I knew it,
I was asleep.

Chapter
FIVE

I was woken to the sound of my name and a light tapping on my arm.

'Isadora,' Mum was whispering. 'Time to wake up!'

I opened my eyes and looked around. For a moment I couldn't remember where I was.

'It's time to go home!' said Mum. 'It's

almost morning!'

I sat up and yawned.

'Is this your friend?' asked Mum,
gesturing at Araminta who was waking up
next to me.

'Yes!' I said, 'Araminta! She's half vampire, half human!'

'You two must have a lot in common then!' said Mum, smiling.

'We do!' I said. 'We're going to be pen pals!'

'Definitely!' said Araminta. 'And maybe one day you could come and visit me where I live?'

'I think that's a very good idea,' said Mum, putting my cape back round my shoulders. She held out her hand and I took it.

'Bye Araminta!' I said, waving.

'Goodbye Isadora.'

Mum and I walked towards the great

front doors of the castle where Dad was waiting. I could see that the sky outside was already lightening and the stars were beginning to disappear.

'What a fantastic night!' Dad said, taking my other hand.

'Really magical!' said Mum.

We stepped into one of the sleek, black taxis waiting outside, and I sank back into the velvet seats. Pink Rabbit curled up next to me. The engine spluttered into life and I felt the car rise up into the air. Dad began to tell the taxi driver all about my performance.

'It was magnificent,' he said. 'We felt so proud! I'm even thinking of learning a little ballet myself now.'

'Did you enjoy yourself, Isadora?' asked Mum as we soared away from the vampire castle, over the craggy mountains and shimmering winding rivers. 'Are you glad you did your ballet show in the end?'

'Oh yes!' I said, remembering how amazing it had felt to dance in front of such a big audience with my new friend Araminta. 'It was the best night ever! I want to do it all again next year!'

Turn the page
for some
Isadorable
things to make
and do!

Star biscuits

Be star of the show with these
delicious star biscuits!

Ingredients

For biscuits:

* 100g unsalted butter, softened at room temperature
* 100g caster sugar
* 1 free-range egg, lightly beaten
* 1 tsp vanilla extract
* 275g plain flour

For decoration:

* 400g icing sugar
* 3-4 tbsp water
* 2-3 drops food colouring
* Edible glitter

Equipment:

- Baking tray
- Greaseproof paper
- Mixing bowl
- Wooden spoon
- Fork
- Sieve
- Rolling pin
- Star-shaped biscuit cutters
- Wire rack
- Knife
- A grown-up assistant to help

Method:

1. Preheat the oven to 190°C/Gas 5.

2. Line a baking tray with greaseproof paper.

3. Cream the butter and sugar together in a bowl until pale, light and fluffy.

4. Beat the egg.

5. Add the beaten egg and vanilla extract, a little at a time, until well combined.

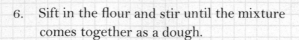

6. Sift in the flour and stir until the mixture comes together as a dough.

7. Lightly flour your clean working surface.

8. Roll the dough out to a thickness of around 1cm.

9. Use the biscuit cutters to cut out star shapes, and carefully place onto the baking tray.

10. Gather the trimmings and repeat steps 8 and 9 until there is no dough left.

11. Bake the biscuits for 8-10 minutes, or until pale golden-brown.

12. Set aside to harden for 5 minutes, then cool on a wire rack.

For the icing:

1. Sift the icing sugar into a large mixing bowl and stir in enough water to create a smooth mixture.

2. Stir in the food colouring (add a tiny amount at a time—a little goes a long way!)

3. Carefully spread the icing onto the biscuits using a knife.

4. Sprinkle over the glitter.

5. Set aside until the icing hardens.

6. Enjoy!

How to make popcorn

If you're putting on a show you do not want a hungry audience to deal with, so why not make them some yummy popcorn?

Make sure a grown up is in charge of the oil, as hot oil is very dangerous.

Ingredients:

★ 1 tbsp sunflower or vegetable oil

★ 50g popcorn kernels

★ Optional toppings: salt, melted butter, Parmesan cheese, cinnamon, anything else you like!

Equipment:

★ Saucepan with lid

★ A grown-up assistant to help

Method:

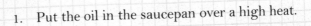

1. Put the oil in the saucepan over a high heat.

2. Put two popcorn kernels into the saucepan, and put the lid on.

3. Wait for the kernels to pop.

4. Take the pan off the heat and remove the popped kernels.

5. Add the rest of the kernels and replace the lid.

6. Shake the saucepan to coat the kernels in the hot oil, and return to the heat. The popcorn should start popping in a couple of minutes.

7. Once the popping slows to 2-3 seconds between pops, remove from the heat.

8. Wait a few extra seconds for the last few pops, then remove the lid.

9. Pour into your popcorn cups (see next page!), removing any unpopped or partially popped kernels you see.

10. Season as you wish.

11. Enjoy!

How to make a popcorn cup

Once you have made your popcorn you
need something for it to go in!
These popcorn cones are perfect.

What you will need:

- Colourful wrapping paper
- Scissors
- Sticky tape

Method:

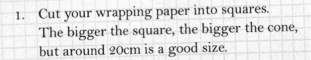

1. Cut your wrapping paper into squares. The bigger the square, the bigger the cone, but around 20cm is a good size.

2. Roll the paper up to create a cone. Make sure you roll it more tightly at one end, so that it doesn't leave a hole. You don't want your popcorn to fall out!

3. Secure the ends of the paper with sticky tape.

4. Put your popcorn in!

Act out a story!

You can do anything when you put on your show: dance, sing, do magic tricks, whatever you're good at. You could even try writing a story that you could act out! Read on for some tips.

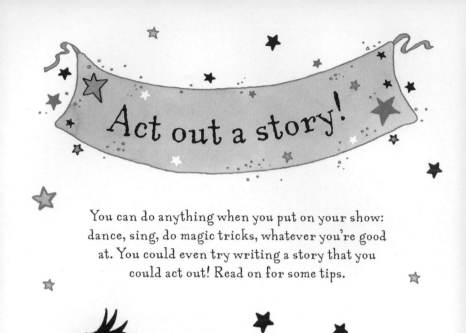

Characters

First you need to decide who your story will be about. Usually stories are about people, but characters can also be animals, magical creatures or even toys that have come to life!

Plot

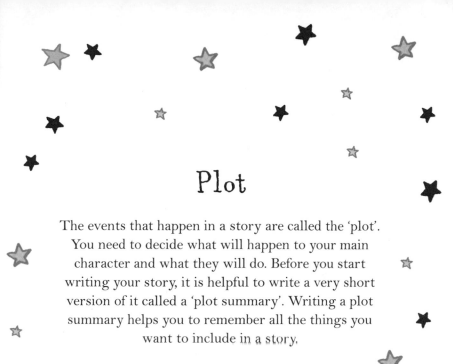

The events that happen in a story are called the 'plot'.
You need to decide what will happen to your main
character and what they will do. Before you start
writing your story, it is helpful to write a very short
version of it called a 'plot summary'. Writing a plot
summary helps you to remember all the things you
want to include in a story.

Problems

Every story needs to have some sort of problem for the main character. The problem can be anything you like, but it has to take some work for the main character to solve.

Easy problems make boring stories. There are a few different ways to make problems more difficult.

1. Didn't work first time

In life, you may not always get something right first time. It's the same in stories. The first thing your character tries might not work for some reason, so they will have to try something else.

2. Obstacles

An obstacle is something which gets in the way.
Obstacles are like mini-problems that make
the main problem worse.

3. Other People Can Be Difficult!

Another person in your story may want or
need or do something that makes things
harder for your character.

Your story might have a villain (or 'baddie')
who makes things difficult on purpose to be
mean, or you might have other characters who
accidentally make things more difficult.

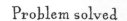

Problem solved

In the final part of the story, you need to show how your
character solves their problem. This will depend on the
type of character and their exact problem.

Here are some questions you could
ask about the solution:

• Did they have to do something, or could
they just talk to someone?

• Did they need a special tool to solve their problem?

• Did they need anyone else to help or did
they do it on their own?

• Was the problem somehow different to
what they thought?

• Is the problem solved forever or just for a while?

Here is a rough outline for how to put
your story together:

Say who your character is and what they are like

↓

Explain what they want or need to do

↓

Describe what problem they have

↓

Show what makes the problem worse

↓

Think of a way for the character to
solve the problem

↓

Tell us what happens at the end

↓

Now you have a story!

How to make a stage

If you're putting on your own show
you need somewhere to do it! Here's how to
make your very own stage at home.

What you will need:

⭐ Two chairs ⭐ A sheet

⭐ A broom ⭐ String

Method:

1. Place your two chairs back to back, about a metre apart.

2. Place the broom over the backs of the two chairs.

3. Pull the chairs apart until around 5cm of your broom handle is hanging over the chair.

4. Secure with string for extra stability.

5. Hang the sheet over the broom handle, so that it touches the floor at the front. This is your stage curtain.

6. At the start of your show come out from behind the curtain!

How to make tickets

To make sure your audience show up at the right time you need to make some tickets! They can be any size or shape, but you need to include the following information:

1. The name of your show. You can call it anything you like, the more exciting the better!

2. The date and time.

3. Where your show is taking place.

How to feel confident

Your stage is set, your audience have snacks, now it's up to you to perform! But sometimes getting up in front of people can be a bit scary. Here are some tips for how to feel confident when you're putting on a show:

1. Stand up straight, look up, and smile! The way you stand really makes a difference to how confident you look, and how confident you feel inside.

2. Practise on your own until you're happy to perform in front of people.

3. If you're feeling nervous, do some belly breathing. Put your hands on your belly and as you breathe slowly in and out imagine a balloon inflating and deflating. This should really help you to calm down.

4. Pretend that your clothes are a protective suit of armour—when you put on your sweater of strength you become a superstar!

5. Remember that nobody is perfect all the time—the only way to improve at something is to keep trying!

6. Don't compare yourself with other people. You are brilliant at being you, nobody does it better!

Training your memory

You have to remember a lot when you're putting on a show, so why not play this game to help train your memory? Look at all the pictures below, then close the book and write down as many as you can remember. Then check back to see if you've forgotten anything!

Where do you belong in a show?

Take the quiz to find out!

When you are on stage in front of people how do you feel?

A. I love performing, it feels amazing!

B. I would much rather watch others than perform myself.

C. If I have written down something to say then I don't mind.

What is your favourite thing to do?

A. Sing and dance.

B. Look after people.

C. I love to make up stories.

If you were dancing in your bedroom and heard a crash downstairs what would you do?

A. I just carry on anyway, the show must go on!

B. I would go and investigate, and try and sort it out.

C. I would make up a story about what could have caused the noise.

Results

Mostly As

You're a born performer, you would be great up on stage!

Mostly Bs

You prefer not to be centre of attention, but that doesn't mean you can't be part of the show! You would be great backstage, making sure that everything runs smoothly.

Mostly Cs

You might not be totally comfortable performing, but you love creating things for other people to perform. You could be a writer, watching at the side of the stage!

Harriet Muncaster

Harriet Muncaster, that's me! I'm the
author and illustrator of Isadora Moon.
Yes really! I love anything teeny tiny,
anything starry, and everything glittery.

Many more magical stories to collect!

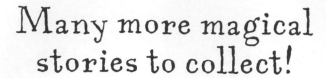

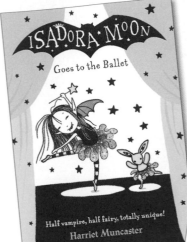

ISADORA MOON
Goes to the Ballet

Half vampire, half fairy, totally unique!
Harriet Muncaster

ISADORA MOON
Has a Birthday

Half vampire, half fairy, totally unique!
Harriet Muncaster

ISADORA MOON
Goes on a School Trip

Half vampire, half fairy, totally unique!
Harriet Muncaster

ISADORA MOON
Gets in Trouble

Half vampire, half fairy, totally [unique!]
Harriet Muncaster

ISADORA MOON
Goes to the Fair

Half vampire, half fairy, totally unique!
Harriet Muncaster

Makes Winter Magic

Plus fangtastic activities!

Half vampire, half fairy, totall...

Harriet

Has a Sleepover

Half vampire, half fairy, totally unique!

Harriet Muncaster

Host your
own magical
Isadora Moon party!

Find a party pack, and lots of
other activities at www.isadoramoon.com

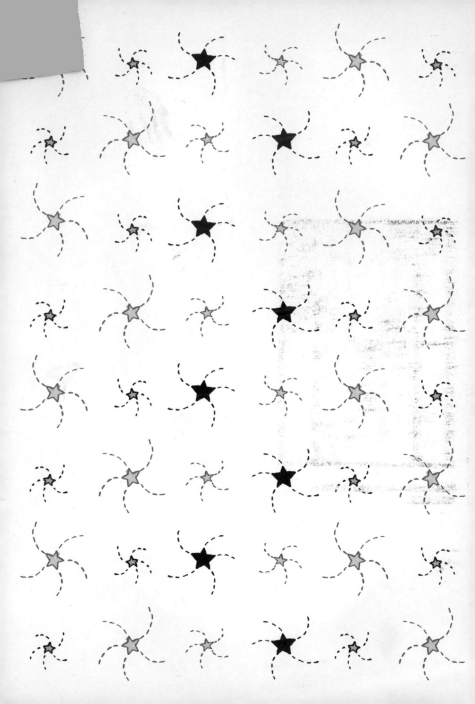